MW01292355

GET OVER A BREAK UP:

THE FIVE STEP GUIDE TO GET OVER YOUR EX, BREAK BAD HABITS AND LEARN TO LOVE YOURSELF

By

Robin Martel

Table of Contents

CHAPTER 1

Intro

When my ex-partner walked out, leaving me a sobbing, broken mess on the living room floor, I felt an influx of panic, anxiety and absolute fear. I could barely breathe or swallow, and my heart felt like it had dropped down to the pit of my stomach, readying itself to lurch right back out of my mouth.

I was scuffled, puffy-faced from crying and laying amongst all of the household items that had been smashed during our enraged argument. Just moments earlier, I was kneeling on the floor with my arms wrapped tightly around my ex's legs, begging him not to leave. Flipping me aside on to the littered floor, he escaped out of the house as quickly as he could.

This was not unusual. Fights were not unusual, physical or verbal. Him leaving me for days and days was not unusual. Me begging him to come back time after time was not unusual. What was unusual, this time, was that I knew I couldn't keep doing this. My heart, absolutely, couldn't take it anymore.

Earlier that evening, things had been pretty typical. I had come home from work, begun making food and opened a bottle of wine to help alleviate the stresses my job often provoked. He was sat watching TV having taken some time off work, and hadn't done anything in the way of housework for a while. He was lazy in that particular sense, and had to be coaxed into doing housework with bribery or promises.

That day was one of those days where I had made a promise in return for some general house tidying whilst I was at work. I had kept my end of the bargain, yet he didn't look like he'd moved from his chair all day. As I poured us both our second glass of wine, I begun to question why no housework had been done. As usual, he got defensive and an argument arose. Again, nothing unusual. We argued a lot.

For a lot of couples, arguments like this are chalked up to being 'petty' or the annoying character traits that their loved ones possess. Often, they are overlooked out of love and are understood to be not that big of a deal in the grand scheme of things.

However, such petty and annoying traits in a partner can cause other underlying feelings to come out and present themselves at any opportunity. My underlying emotions stemmed from being cheated on by my partner and, as I couldn't keep trudging over his past affairs forever, I snapped at him at any other given chance. This time, it was over housework.

What began as a dispute over housework led to the unraveling of our feelings beneath the surface, which always led to highly-strung and volatile arguments. The arguments often lasted hours, sometimes spilling over days. This one escalated quickly, and ended how they did frequently. I was told he no longer loved me before we scuffled at the front door, and he flung my begging body to the side.

As I lay on the cold and uncomfortable wooden floor, I turned onto my back and stared at the ceiling. The sickening thoughts of everything he'd ever done to me washed over my mind. It was times like this, after an argument and him walking out, he would stay at his friend's house, go out drinking all night. It was on these occasions he would cheat. Days would pass, he wouldn't reply to messages, voicemails or any type of pleading from me to come home and work it out. That is, until he was ready to come home and it would always be on his terms.

There would be no mention of the previous few days' mental torture I'd endured, not knowing where he'd been and who he had potentially been with. On the hellish days he would stay away and ignore me, I'd be unable to eat, sleep or function properly. Days at work would be painful and slow, if I managed to go at all.

I found out about and forgave two instances of cheating (using the term forgave loosely – I never did truly forgive him, I was simply scared of losing him). The rest of his affairs came to light after the break-up, which made me feel even more worthless and like I must have somehow asked to be treated in such a way. It also dawned on me how obvious his adulterous behavior had been, and I had been refusing to accept it the whole time. I felt like a prize idiot when I found out, to say the least – although not shocked, which speaks volumes.

Laying amongst broken vases, smashed ornaments and soil from the toppled over houseplants, my heart was broken into a thousand pieces. Thinking back now, the image of myself back then is that of somebody I would love to be able to walk up to, extend my hand out to them and be able to sit them down and talk to them.

To let them know things would be okay (more than okay in fact, although feeling just 'okay' seems like a luxury when going through a serious break-up). To let them know what they're feeling isn't permanent, that they will be happy and the things that they're going through are all part of the process that leads to genuine happiness.

Time and time again I had been betrayed, unheard and cast aside by my ex. Every argument and fight I could remember played out in my head, as did the seemingly dire reality of what my life would now be; single, possibly jobless after numerous days off sick and struggling to cope financially.

I lay with tears streaming from my face and into my hair, pleading the question "why?" - *why* wasn't I wanted? *Why* do I have to feel like this?

As much as I yearned for my ex, I knew deep down it was a horrible fear of abandonment that lead me to accept such low standards and kept me going through this same old rigmarole. The thoughts of being alone and nobody ever wanting me began to seep into my mind.

I had to get him out of my system and get over this break-up. I was fine before we met and I'll be fine again. I told myself these things over and over until I cried myself to sleep.

I awoke feeling the same as I always did the day after he broke up with me. Like I said, he did this often; every few months or so. Sick, anxious, needy and unable to talk properly were some of the side effects of him leaving. The only way I could quell these feelings was to have him with me, at home, just holding me. Even then, the fear of him leaving again and again, until he eventually did it for good, was enough to drive me to insanity.

This time, however, I was going to go cold turkey.

I wouldn't text, call or email. I wouldn't try and see what he was doing on social media. I wouldn't spend my days sobbing and wondering what was so wrong with me. Needy, pathetic me was going to have to go, for good. Regardless of my emotions toward him, or my want to just have him be with me, I couldn't allow another human being to treat me with such little regard or respect.

I can admit to not being perfect in our relationship – I could often be picky, take my work stresses out on him and be very introverted at times. These things he found difficult, as I'm sure many partners would. However, the counteractive treatment he served me because of my 'shortcomings' was nothing less than torture for my heart. I knew I needed to let go.

But how?

I'm going to take my experiences, using the heartbreaks I have endured, and show you how you can get over your ex and triumph over heartbreak. As well as this, I can show you how to take your heartbreak and use it to make yourself the best version of yourself; think of the little caterpillar transforming itself into the wondrous butterfly. This break-up is your cocoon.

Unlike the mysterious happenings inside the cocoon of a soon-to-be butterfly, I can show you exactly how to transform from where you are now (and where I once was) to where you ought to be; where you need to be and deserve to be. I've lived through utter heartbreak and I am here to show you how to come out of the other side, not only better, but the *best.*

Coupling my own experiences with my knowledge of the human psyche, I can offer the most compassionate and knowledgeable advice to aid you in getting over a break-up. This isn't a '48-hour cure' or some lame offering that cites knowledge from a textbook to give you scientific heartbreak cures. I will lay down the foundations so you know just what surviving a break-up entails, then help you build yourself back up using the same techniques that I (and many others) have used.

CHAPTER 2

Grieving and Healing – What you are feeling now, what you're going to feel and why you need to feel it: The Seven Stages of Grieving an Ex

There's no two ways about it: you *will* feel dreadful emotional pain during the process of getting over your ex. It will feel like there's no other pain in the world that matters. In fact, it may hurt so much you swear you can feel it physically. You may feel like there is a bottomless pit of hurt, anger, desperation and questions and you're just falling helplessly into this black pit of heartbreak. It's hard to imagine when you're tumbling through the black hole that these feelings will ever go away.

To help you better understand the process you're going through, I've dedicated a whole chapter explaining what's going to happen and what you will feel during each stage. You'll likely recognize which Stage you're currently at and I'll help you prepare for what's next.

Stage One: Desperation

Desperation and fixation is the beginning stage of a break-up. I recall my 'Stage One' vividly, as I endured it many times throughout my two serious relationships. Combined, these two relationships took up well over a decade of my life – that's a long time to suffer the helpless feeling of desperation.

During this phase, you may be desperate to know why the break-up occurred, why you deserve to be feeling the way you do or you may be yearning to know why you simply aren't wanted anymore. There are numerous 'why's' that you will be asking, and the answers will seem so far away from your grasp right now.

During your 'Stage One' process, you (just like I did), may begin to fixate on things of the past; old conversations, events and broken promises that may hide clues to the demise of your relationship. If you can access those clues, you tell yourself you can maybe find a way to rectify the wrongdoing that killed your relationship and ignite that fire that was once there.

This stage of the grieving and healing process is one of the hardest to go through. But trust me, once you begin making your way through these seven steps, you are getting stronger and stronger at each pass – no matter how weak you feel or how close to giving up you think you are.

The sheer weight of desperation during this phase fogs your mind. Your vision of your ex becomes very rose tinted. They are the only person that can break you free from your anguished prison, yet they are the one who locked you in there (although during my very last 'Stage One', I realized this isn't true. It was ME who had locked myself in there and it was only ME who could free myself from my anguished prison).

Fundamentally, this stage can turn you into a big, answer-seeking mess. During my break-up with my first serious relationship, I suffered in silence. I didn't tell anyone, I didn't talk to anyone and I kept it all inside. A big part of this was that very few people knew we were together; it was a physically abusive relationship (yes, I sure know how to pick them) and friends and family were unhappy about me continuously returning to him, even after numerous trips to hospital and many days in hiding until black eyes and bruises had gone.

Because of the relationship being mostly secret, I had no one to talk to. If you currently have no one to talk to, you may be like I was; asking rhetorical questions in your head, spending hours upon hours going over old messages, living inside your head, sobbing alone. I can tell you from experience (and you may know this already), that this is absolutely unhealthy. Even if you are choosing not to talk to anybody because you don't want to, keeping things bottled inside will only cause you to implode with the energy sucking emotion that drives your desperation.

Instead of keeping things tightly contained, I would highly recommend the following:

- Write your thoughts and feelings down. Even if you don't want to keep them or think it's 'silly' to do so. You can always get it down on paper, read it back to yourself and then rip the paper up (or burn it in my case. I had penned a letter to my ex that I found stuffed in a drawer. I think I was roughly at Stage Six when I found it after hiding it away during Stage One. Although it reminded me of how I had felt, and brought a little pain back, it also reaffirmed to me how far I had come and how much further I can go. I even smiled after I had read it; partly due to the cringe worthy content, mostly because I was proud of me).

- Speak aloud. Again, you may feel stupid, but you'll feel less weighed once you have decompressed and let your desperation out. Whatever is going through your head – say it! I had my trusty Jack Russell who would listen to me as I explained my feelings, questioned why I was going through this pain and expressing my loss at what to do next. Although you may think it's odd to talk to your dog (don't worry – I wasn't expecting a response from him), getting my thoughts and feelings out of my system did help me declutter my mind and feel slightly better. If you're lacking a dog, simply talk aloud. You WILL feel better.

The Stage One of my second break-up was much different. This time, I didn't keep it all in. I would cry to friends and family, ask them questions about their thoughts on what I did so wrong, what I needed to do next and ask them to debate my failings with me. I was lucky enough to have one friend who had also recently split from his boyfriend and was also taking it hard. He would come around to my house and we would spill our guts for hours. Sometimes when he left I would feel worse, but knowing what I know now, it was something I needed to do in order to overcome my (as I now know it) Stage One and break through this gut churning break-up.

Stage One – and remember this – like all the Seven Stages, can only last so long.

The desperation and fixation on things period certainly takes its toll, however. This means your fragile mind will need to find a way to fix this, and will eventually move on to the next Stage of the grieving and healing process – denial.

Stage Two – Denial

It's not true. You were both in love. He's/she's made a huge mistake and just doesn't realize it yet! This relationship is NOT over – it's just a tremulous period that will have to come to an end because you belong to each other. You truly know this. Sound like you? Then welcome to Stage Two – Denial.

Although I know you won't necessarily be actually 'welcoming' any of these Stages, once your grieving process is over, I can tell you that you'll look back and be proud of how far you've came and just how much strength you truly have. You really will surprise yourself in the best possible way – especially later on in the book, where I share with you the same methods, steps to happiness and habits of self-care that I adopted to ensure I became a much better version of myself (and found the love of my life, but more on that later).

For now, any of the above may seem miles away, if attainable at all. In fact, it's highly likely you don't want to move on right now, you just want to be with your ex. I was the same – we all are. It's happened to me, it's happening to you and it'll happen to people as long as the world is turning.

Switching from desperation to denial gives your overactive mind a break. It ensures you stop asking questions, pleading with yourself for answers and fixating on your loss. It allows your mind to rest.

Your mind is now counteracting the desperation of Stage One and filling it with hope in Stage Two, in the form of denial. This is a case of your mind 'playing tricks', however.

The purpose of denial is to prevent you from feeling anymore emotional pain and is your mind's way of helping you avoid more distress.

So whilst your mind is trying to be helpful and give you some feelings of hope and reassurance, you need to know that this is simply a phase of the Seven Stages and isn't a true reflection of where your relationship with your ex is.

Think of it as a mirage; you're in an unbearably hot desert, surrounded by miles upon miles of scorching hot sand. All of a sudden you see a sparkling oasis in the distance, with the water shining bright sunlight reflections into your eyes. The elation you feel when you see hope of water and comfort in the distance would be enough to spur you on further in your plight.

It's the same with Stage Two of your grieving process. Denial is your mind's very own 'mirage' that is there to give you a renewed sense of hope and offers a place to channel all of your emotions. So, whilst your mind thinks it's being helpful, it's in fact just a detour from facing reality.

I have, many times, used denial to maintain my horrendous past relationships. I would argue that we were meant to be, that the years we have spent together mean too much to throw away.

Obviously none of that was true, although I didn't know that then. Getting stuck at Stage Two was often my downfall. I'd use my denial-driven sales pitch and tell my ex exactly why we shouldn't split up. Inevitably, we'd stay together. Low and behold, I'd find myself repeating the same situation time after time (which is also known as Stage Four – Relapse. My arch nemesis for many, many years. More on that in a bit).

Whilst your situation may be different, as all of our break-up circumstances are, the element of denial still rears its ugly head regardless of the separation conditions.

Denial leads to Stage Three – bargaining. This is driven by denial so it is the natural next step in the process.

Stage Three – Bargaining

You're currently at the edge of a chasm and are doing anything you can to avoid going down there. You're doing everything in your power to cling on to the known and avoid stepping into the unknown, which is (often unfortunately) the makings of human nature.

This next step of avoidance ensures us heartbroken folk aren't leaving this without a fight. From the classic promises of how much you'll be better this time round to even offering conditions that you aren't comfortable with, it's all in aid of keeping this 'special someone' with you.

If you put me in front of a potential customer and told me to sell a product, I'd be a bumbling halfwit; giving nonsensical reasons for them to buy the product and generally having no real clue what I was doing. Selling is just something I'd be uncomfortable doing and don't have the knack of.

However, if you imagine me all those years ago, giving my exes my bargaining sales pitch, I was a maestro at selling. I'd spew the reasons they ought to be with me and offer them the benefits of returning to the relationship like a pro saleswoman. I'd sell myself until I was back in the comfort of that relationship (although, as I know now, it was always just a temporary comfort – I was too scared to go it alone and feel the dreadful things I'd need to in order to become truly happy).

Heartbreak and the agony of separation can really ensure all logic is thrown out of the window. This might be a good time to mention that it's best not to make any big choices whilst you are going through this time in your life. I got myself into a heavy amount of debt during my last break-up. Whilst this may seem small time in comparison to those who really do extreme things when making their way through heartbreak, it's still more stress added onto an already extremely stressful (to say the least) situation. Where possible, try and have a few moments thought and clarity (ways of how to do this are offered later in the book) before embarking on anything major.

Back to bargaining – the Stage Three phase of your break-up. Whilst you're here, remember to note that you *are* making progress, regardless of how you feel.

Getting back to the psychology of the bargaining phase, much like the Stage Two period of denial, your mind is acting as a distraction from facing the reality of loss and the anxiety of separation. Bargaining has you adopting the mindset of winning him/her back, at any cost. You'll even be willing to take the blame for everything that contributed to the demise of the relationship.

By bargaining, you're trying to take control of something that has rendered you powerless. You're taking responsibility for the end of your relationship and begin giving yourself the illusion that by doing so, you can fix it. And by any means necessary! The sheer grit and determination you gain during this phase of breaking up can astounding. By allowing yourself to perceive that the relationship is salvageable, you are putting off feeling the sheer devastation of loss.

Bargaining, as I am especially all too aware, leads to Stage Four – relapsing. You may or may not relapse, as you may have no choice in the matter if your ex is sticking tightly to their guns and not getting back with you. This, although you likely don't see or feel it now, is a positive for you in your heartbreak journey to happiness.

Stage Four – Relapse

If you are like I was, it may be a case of relapsing (plural) than a singular relapse. I did it time and time again, somehow each time convincing myself that this time it will work out.

If relapse isn't an option for you, you're one of the lucky ones. I'm aware you'll be reading this and pondering how so, when all you want is to be back in the arms of your ex. But trust me, by this stage not being made available to you, your ex is doing you a serious time-saving favor.

I felt, and in all probability, you feel, that the only way to quash the pain is to be with your ex. This gives you a temporary (stressing the word *temporary*) feeling of elation, then the comfortable feeling of safety. However, you are only prolonging the emotional distress even more by giving into makeshift comfort.

I would feel so euphoric when I was finally back in the arms of my ex, regardless of what he had done to me. Just to feel safe and loved and like things could just be better and nicer from now on gave me a short-term feeling of happiness. I literally had withdrawals when we were apart, so when he agreed each time to give it another go (given that I abide by his newly enforced terms and conditions), I felt somewhat 'me' again. My panic attacks would subside and I could sleep better, believing that I was loved and cared for.

This was the worst thing I could do. And if this sounds like you, I have some harsh truths for you (that you will look back on in a couple of months' time and #1 agree with me and #2 be glad you heard them).

You can't carry the relationship alone, nor can you be responsible for the burden of everything that goes wrong in the relationship. For someone else to allow you to do this more than indicates that they don't truly care for your wellbeing.

Reconciling more than once is the norm for us broken hearted ones. I recall a friend of mine asking me, "how many times do you need to make the same mistake before you learn" when I returned to my cheating ex. Such a simple question that she probably thought nothing more of after asking me it. However, it got to me and I did think about the answers to that question. So, if you are in the same routine of relapsing like I was, have a think about that question and ponder your answers to it. Just for a few moments.

How many times do you need to make the same mistake before you learn?

If you are on the other end of the relapsing spectrum, and are being coaxed back to your relationship by your ex (even though you know it's only going to crash and burn), the above question still applies.

Before I hit Stage Five – the resentment phase – I relapsed more times than I care to remember. During my decade (and then some) of two bad relationships, I hit double figures with my relapses. Perhaps I just needed to know the relationship was a dud for *sure* (rolling my eyes as I write this). I am the type who will work at something to ensure the best outcome, however I was damaging my health and happiness in the long run with my constant relapses.

More than this, I was feeding my attachment issues by not looking into the true reasons I couldn't be apart from my then-lovers. It was only when I did this, that I realized that if I didn't change, then neither would my situation.

It was during a relapse that we argued about something irrelevant, then he up and left me laying on the floor (a sobbing heap, if you recall). It was those days after that I knew that I had to stop repeating this same demeaning behavior. I had to take control of myself and my life. Those awful days I laid in bed, didn't eat and broke out in cold sweats constantly. But – I was adamant that I was going to get through this, somehow, someway. And it all began with taking control.

Your reading of this book suggests you are at that point too, which can often be a very difficult place to get to. Change isn't something us humans are particularly accommodating to, especially when it comes to matters of the heart.

Once we pass through the Stage Four process of relapsing, we will enter the new phase of emotions. Resentment is an ugly word that is used to describe even uglier feelings, and that is what you will feel next.

Stage Five – Resentment

Whilst the feelings are ugly, it's a good thing to feel resentment during this time. It means you're in the midst of taking back control and taking that grey cloud over your head and turning it into thunder. Again, that might sound bad – but your anger and resentment are going to empower you.

Up until now, you could only connect with feelings of despair, desperation and loss. You have been thrust into the unknown, which naturally evokes feelings of fear and anxiety. Up until this point you have felt immobilized with your emotions, knowing only dread and anxiety. Despair and desperation were winning the war of emotions, trumping all others with ease.

As you progress through the seven stages, as I mentioned earlier, it's important to remember that they will all pass in time. You may think I'm spinning you a cliché and that next I'll be telling you how a 'smooth sea never made a skilled sailor' (very true – I do like that expression) amongst other pick-me-up phrases. I'm sure you've been given enough sympathetic looks accompanying those types of phrases lately, but some of them are very true and insightful – I've popped a few of my favorites at the end of the book to give you a boost and some food for thought. Hopefully, like me, they'll provide some comfort that you are now in charge of your own fate.

Returning to resentment, this can take shape in a few ways. It all depends on your own personality, temperament, how screwed over you feel or pretty much just your own set of separation circumstances. You may feel anger at the situation, your ex, yourself, your family. Misdirected or not, this resentment is the fuel you will use to power yourself through this tormented time. It's ironic that a misdirection of feelings can somehow be the guide pointing you in the right direction, allowing you to feel more awakened to the situation.

Like the majority of us broken hearted, you're probably aiming a lot of that anger and resentment at yourself. Defeatist and counteractive could be what you are thinking; however, I disagree – you are no longer the lifeless pit of emotions you were a few stages back. You are now hurtling through the grieving process and have come so far. By this point in your progress through the Stages, you have hosted enough hurt, anger and discomfort inside of you that you are able to use that to shift your way of thinking. Perspectives change and proactivity is something within reach at this point now.

Of course, you're only human; even during my Stage Five, I had bad days. I still had days where it all got a bit much, and I would excuse myself from social situations to go home and lay down alone and in silence. However, these days were getting fewer and fewer, and more to the point, I was actively putting myself in social situations now. I recall a meal out with friends one afternoon and I just sat quiet, barely ate, offered nothing but my physical presence. I was having a bad day. But even just getting ready, heading out and socializing was something I couldn't even think of a few Stages ago.

And more encouragingly, I began laughing and smiling again. I was finding jokes funny, I was enjoying television and began reading again. Resentment and anger were still very much there, but their presence became less and less. Amongst the anger and frustration, I was becoming human again.

Time was passing and I would go fifteen minutes without a thought for my ex. Then half an hour, then an hour, then a whole three hours without a thought for my ex! Days passed and I began proactively seeking alternative things to keep myself occupied. Whether it was binge watching whole seasons of sitcoms, going to meet friends and drink lots of wine and find my sense of humor again or begin making homemade bracelets – I was keeping busy and find new parts of me at the same time.

Understandably, throughout this I would have moments of wishing I was partaking in these activities with my ex, or that I was able to travel back in time to when we were together and happy. Sometimes it would hit me like a ton of bricks. However, fueled by my newfound passionate feelings of resentment, I was ready to make more changes.

By this point, it's ready to move on to Stage Six – the beginnings of acceptance.

Stage Six – The Beginnings of Acceptance

By this point, you are still grieving. You're very much here because you have to be and not because you want to be. And that's okay. Because by this point, you have been through enough and generated enough emotions to conclude the following:

It's no good for you to keep trying any longer.

And it's such a wonderful feeling to know that you have developed enough thought for yourself and enough awareness of your situation that you can now think this way.

Boundaries are being stuck to because it's for your own self-care. The want for contact will be nowhere near as bad as it was a few Stages ago; it will be fleeting by this point. Still, controlling the impulse for contact must be avoided.

I recall my ex emailing me whilst I began my foray into Stage Six. It was for something silly, like some paperwork that he so desperately needed, months after we had last spoken. I knew he didn't need this paperwork, in fact it was something that was easily printed off of the internet and he knew I knew this.

He wanted contact. After ending it with me, treating me with such disdain during our break-up and leaving me in pieces, he now decided he wanted contact. Just as I was gaining control of my life again.

I didn't reply. I didn't reply to the next two emails asking if I had gotten the first, then asking how I was doing. I didn't accept the attempt at messages on social media. Only when he emailed again, this time when I was in a new relationship, did I reply to firmly but politely. I told him yes, I did get the emails, but I wish to have no correspondence.

The point of me telling you this, is that I had now mustered enough willpower not to message or be sucked into replying. That's not to say I didn't at times draft up a response to say how much he'd hurt me; the main takeaway is the fact that I didn't reply. And I couldn't have been prouder of me. I was accepting that it was no good for me to keep trying any longer.

You will have many defining moments during this Stage. You will have moments where you surprise yourself and abstain from doing the damaging things you were doing only just a few Stages ago. That could be stopping yourself sending texts or posting Facebook statuses that you hope will evoke jealousy in your ex. It could be talking yourself out of staying in and hiding away, it could be reminding yourself of the things that went wrong in your relationship.

With your mind now in acceptance mode, you will feel your cocoon slowly loosening around your new self, readying yourself to break free of this heartbreak prison.

Stage Seven is awaiting you, and it's the most wonderful sense of achievement.

Stage Seven – Renewed Hope

When your relationship died, so did hope.

Hope was replaced with panic, dread and desperation. The jarring feeling of initial acceptance allows your reserves of hope to rise up to the surface again. Even when you believe your last glimmer of hope has gone, be comforted by the fact that hope is always within you and know that it's part of why us humans are so resilient. Don't doubt your own resilience.

Renewed hope means you can now see a future for yourself without your ex in it. You can envision yourself in a week, month, two months' time and know you're going to be okay. In fact, more than okay – you know you'll be happy, free and excited at the prospects you are going to create for yourself.

My defining Stage Seven moment occurred a few days after I seen my ex whilst out shopping. He was with someone else, and I was with a friend of mine. My heart lurched into my throat and I tried my best to avoid him. I was semi successful, but I knew he saw me and continued to look when he thought I couldn't see. Stages earlier, this would have broken me. I would have felt physically sick.

But now, I really just wanted to avoid him and get on with some retail therapy. And once he was out of my sight, I breathed a sigh of relief and continued with my day. I worried that this would have a two-steps-back effect on me. I had a date the next evening and was worried it would cause some sort of delayed adverse reaction during our date.

It didn't. My date and I got on very well. We drank, we laughed, we mocked each other's unfamiliar accents and actually got deep in emotional conversation. Not something that usually occurs on a first date, but we had similar backgrounds, with our difficult childhoods and just-as-tough relationships.

After a fleeting try at romance, we became friends. He went on to meet a lovely girl shortly after and (as far as I'm aware) is very happy.

But it was after this date, and the lack of anything meaningful developing from it, that I knew I was full of renewed hope and a real lust for life without my ex was emerging.

It was amazing. And when this feeling arrives at your feet, I hope you remember your time reading this book and recall how elated I told you you'd feel.

Interlude

Before we begin the next chapter, I want to offer a quick interlude. I'll do this a few times throughout the book to offer you some simple affirmations I want you to reiterate to yourself. Affirmations are important when overcoming such a traumatic event in your life, as your mind can easily cloud over all logic and leave you lost without a clear thought to cling on to.

With these interludes, I would like you to take a couple of minutes and either think or say these affirmations out loud. Occasionally, like this affirmation, I will need you to finish the end of the sentence.

Repeat this ten times.

"I am better off without my ex because..."
I can finally wear that top I love but he hated, I can read before bed without 'neglecting' him, I can be late home and not be yelled at, I can speak to a member of the opposite sex without feeling guilty, I can begin to live my life in a way I choose, I can begin to seek out a better life...

Whatever your 'because' may be, repeat it. Reaffirm it in your mind. Let your reasons tumble from your mind out of your mouth.

All of the affirmations scattered throughout this book are compiled at the very end, if you wish to do all at once or memorize them.

CHAPTER 3

Zero Contact, Social Media & The Cold Turkey Way

It's a trap all of us heartbroken ones have eagerly jumped into at some point, or throughout, turbulent relationships and break-ups – contacting our ex-spouses, regardless of whether it is welcomed or not. There are three main ways this can happen, either directly or indirectly. I'll address all three individually: in person, on the phone and via social media. Us devastated ones will usually take full advantage of all three until we finally decide to take our happiness into our own hands. Admittedly, it took me a while to go cold turkey, but I did it. Because of this, I know you can too. Here's how:

Contact Via Phone

Providing you're not blocked or haven't deleted their number, it's likely you are, in your vulnerable and lonely state, sending lots of unrequited text messages or Whatsapp messages. To combat unanswered messages, you may be dozens of phone calls to your ex. Of course, these are likely to be ignored or declined – I know the sinking feeling all too well. The persistent and impatient side of me would show itself whenever this happened, and I would counteract every declined call with a redial. This would either lead to the contact I had been yearning for, or being blocked.

If you are seeing parts of yourself in my behavior, hopefully I can make you see that you're not crazy or psychotic. You are hurt and are reacting to your feelings. But, cold turkey is the *only* way you will get over this tough time in your life. As hard as it is, and as difficult you may find it to accept, it is the only way.

My trick to abstaining from calling or texting? Turning my phone off and leaving it away from me.

Obviously, I had to muster up the willpower to do this, and at times found it an annoyance when I was conversing with friends or needing to make a call elsewhere. But I knew I had to let this powerful urge pass, and it wouldn't disappear if my phone was so easily accessible.

Switching my phone off and leaving it in my work drawer or on my bedside table and leaving it alone ensured I let the overwhelming urge to contact my ex pass. If I was at work I would actively throw myself into my job to take my mind off texting. Even if it was a quiet day in the office, I would find something to do – take on a side project, clear my desk or even help out stuffing envelopes.

By turning my phone off, I took back control. I wasn't looking at my phone every few minutes, hoping he would have replied to a message or decided to call me back.

Here are some things to remember when you are thinking of picking up the phone...

#1 Why should you have to convince anyone to be with you? Whatever relationship-salvaging sales pitch you have in your head, you need to mentally crumple it up and throw it in your minds bin. You are better than arguing and pleading yourself back into a relationship.

#2 Let's say you do call. Either your ex will answer, or they won't. If they don't, you are left anxiously wondering what to do and watching the clock so you can give it another painstaking go in a few moments. If they do answer, it likely won't go how you imagined it in your head. They might be busy and need to hang up, leaving you in a state of confusion. They may answer angrily, sick of your persistence, and say some hurtful things to reject your contact. Or, they may pick up and the conversation does actually go pretty well...but they don't want to see you, and are just politely declining your attempts at contact. Regardless of the outcome, you'll be ending the phone call upset, angry and frustrated.

#3 It allows you to be picked up and put back down again as they please. Should they be at a loose end and you call, you run the huge risk of being used. You are a human being, not a form of entertainment for someone else. If you are in the frame of mind where this option sounds better than not seeing them at all (oh, I've felt this. My self-esteem and value for myself were beyond ground down), then remind yourself of the feeling you'll get when you're dumped again. Should you allow yourself to be used like this, you may feel reconnected for a short while, but reality will set back in. This person has made you feel utter despair, you should refrain from offering them yourself any longer.

#4 They aren't the ones calling you. If they wanted to call, they would. As hard as this is to hear, you need to hear it to remind yourself not to devalue yourself – you are better and tougher than this situation.

#5 You are literally wasting valuable time. The time you spend chasing your ex on the phone (or anywhere else in fact) is time you could be spent on yourself. Your free time should be focusing on you, your health and happiness. Reevaluate and spend time thinking about you, where you'd like to be in life and what dreams you've yet to achieve. Swap thoughts of phone conversations to thoughts of you, what you're going to do this evening, is there anything you forgot to do today, are you behind on anything at work... I found getting lost in film and books initially helped as a distraction, which in turn opened my mind further.

In Person

You know before you even do it – you're putting yourself in the absolute firing line by turning up at your ex's home or place of work. As romantic as the idea may seem in your head, turning up to either be ignored or rejected is humiliating. Perhaps you were even going to take gifts, or some old clothes you thought 'they might need' to seem a little warmer to them.

As endearing and cute as those things are in your head, the harsh truth is that you are not only demeaning yourself, you are open to looking a little unhinged (especially if you're turning up at their place of work – trust me, I've been there too).

I have sobbed at my ex's door begging them to see me, I've shown up at their work on their lunch and caught them when I knew they'd be outside having a cigarette. I bore gifts, old keepsakes that I thought would bring them back to me – so trust me when I say you really need to refrain yourself from doing this. Even if every fiber of your being wants to, you need to rationalize.

If they wanted to see you, they would.

You wouldn't need to be stood outside knocking on their door when you know they are home, or purposefully 'bumping into' them. Even if you simply want to stop by their house and post a letter to them – don't. You are professing your love to someone who clearly doesn't deserve it if they would allow you to go to such lengths, only to let you be hurt again.

If you have their mail still being delivered at yours, don't hand deliver it to their new address, or stop by their parents to leave it there. Simply write 'return to sender' on the envelope and place in the post box. You'll surprise yourself at how empowering that actually feels.

Social Media

A clean break when social media is involved seems highly unlikely these days. Social media stalking after a break-up isn't seen by the masses as something unhealthy, and popular culture even encourages it.

It's very normal, that's true. But it is also vitally unhealthy and a major hindrance to you getting over this break-up, and becoming the person you owe it to yourself to be.

Of course, you're going to look. You going to want to see where they've been, who they've been with, how happy they look and try and spot any clues that they may be missing you. Stalking an ex via social media can be almost addictive – you get an initial rush of euphoria, but like all drugs, there is a comedown.

Whether your comedown is because they're looking good, have been having a good time or simply because their posts have reminded you of why you loved them so much – your comedown isn't going to feel good. That horrible feeling in the pit of your stomach that arises when you lurk on your ex partner's social media pages is something

45

you *can* control; you need a little willpower and enough love for yourself to stop putting yourself through that. This little book will guide you to loving yourself, but you need to want it first.

So, here is my little guide to the use of social media after breaking up:

Relationship status

If your ex hasn't already changed this, take the bold step of removing them from your relationship status. If they have got in there before you and removed the status, consider it a gesture to spur you on in your quest for closure; they've made it clear there's no going back and you'll stick to that.

If your ex still has the status on there, they may just be leaving it for a few days to soften the blow to you or avoid any awkward questions from their friends or family. They may also be leaving their relationship status as it is to leave the door open slightly; maintaining their relationship with you as their back-up plan.

It doesn't matter which of the two scenarios above reflect your ex partner's reasons for keeping their relationship status, I would recommend being the one to take it down. Not only can this feel empowering, you are also taking back control. You aren't allowing yourself to be open to the manipulative methods your ex could be using.

Pictures and posts

Delete or keep? That is entirely up to you, and initially you will be understandably hesitant to delete your memories. Deleting old pictures and posts may seem like you're ripping pages out of a diary, and it may be heartbreaking for you to erase them.

As time goes by, you *will* meet somebody new. Although this all seems so far away at the moment, if possible at all, please keep in mind that you do have a future; would you care that the person you're going to marry could see soppy posts, pictures and cute little messages to your ex?

I get that you possibly feel nothing from this prospect right now, and hasty deletions can do more harm than good. But be prepared for a spring clean; you'll know when the time is right to begin that process.

I recall the feeling of empowerment I had when I came to my social media spring clean. I felt like my future was in my hands, and that I had cleared the path for greater things. It's funny how such a seemingly small thing can really give you a boost towards becoming you again.

Refrain from the negative posting

Under this umbrella includes cryptic posting and song lyrics. Both will translate as: "please ask about my breakup".

Also included under this heading is the "having such a great time", "life is so good right now", "happiest that I've ever been" posts or pictures – not only will your friends and followers know you're not genuine, you'll also have your breakthrough moment in this break-up and go back and delete them out of embarrassment. Avoid posting them in the first place, although I understand it can be hard when your ex appears to be fine without you. It's only natural to want to counter that with your own showing of happiness – but don't do it unless it's the real deal.

Comments and posts that are derogatory towards your ex are also to be avoided – regardless of how hurt you are or the terrible things they've done to you. Not only will you seem bitter, it's not worth your energy in the much grander scheme of things.

Using others to spy

If you've taken the plunge by deleting your ex off your social media, or have been blocked by them, it can be tempting to ask your friends to be your own personal Jessica Fletcher and go do some digging on your behalf.

I have been here, too; occasionally my friends and I would gather round and we'd take a look at what my ex had been getting up to. Although my friends would try and make me feel better about it by pointing out his shortfalls or offering witty digs about him, I'm not sure my fake laughter hid the fact that seeing him happy without me made me die inside.

The key takeaway from this is no matter how badly you want to spy or use others to help you do so, it's all to your own detriment. You won't come away feeling better, and it'll make darn sure that your thoughts are heavily occupied with your ex for the foreseeable. To really break free from the shackles of a break-up, you need to muster the willpower to avoid doing these small yet destructive actions.

Interlude

Take a moment to find some clarity. Put the book down, close your eyes and imagine somewhere you've always wanted to go, something you've always wanted to do or even just put yourself in a place that makes you feel safe. Repeat the following short, yet deeply true phrase. You can say it out loud, whisper it or just keep it in your head – whatever works for you.

I want to be happy. I deserve to be happy.

You can also add a 'because' section to the end of that statement to really give your affirmation some juice for your mind. The more you affirm to yourself that you want to be happy and you deserve happiness in abundance, the more your mind will attract that for you. The more you dwell in the pity and angst of your break-up, the more your mind will seek out negativity and ill emotions (like looking at their social media or texting them).

Three Methods to Maintain Zero Contact

Willpower doesn't just arrive at your feet when you need it – if it did, we'd all have such an easier time during a break-up!

Instead, we need to work on mustering that willpower and gravitating it towards us. Here are three proven methods to help you assemble all the willpower you'll need to maintain zero contact with your ex.

#1 Beware The White Bear

Although it sounds like a nursery rhyme you can't really remember, 'beware the white bear' is something you should keep in mind when trying not to think about contacting your ex.

It's psychologically proven; the more you try to not think about something, the more you actually do think about that certain something. So, if you try to not think of a white bear, what do you suppose you're constantly thinking of? ... *A white bear!*

Your ex is a temptation and like all forbidden temptations, the more you try to not think of it, the more it lures you in. Picture a dieter obsessing over the chocolate cake in the fridge - because they're constantly trying not to think about going to eat it, they're constantly thinking about going to eat it.

The exercise here is to not beat yourself up about your ex racking your brain; don't take it as a sign, don't be the dieter giving in to that cake!

#2 Admire someone else

I don't mean fall into the arms of another person or start drooling over new people you meet ... this means find a new role model.

It can be someone you admire from afar, someone you're just getting to know or a celebrity. If they share something in common with you, have been through similar experiences and they are living a life that looks admirable to you – go catch some of their good energy!

Science shows us that we can soak up willpower from other people; they can strengthen our determination and spur us on in our darkest moments, if they or something they have done can resonate with us.

My break-up role model was a celebrity. Throughout their life, they had shown strength, guts, resilience and after every setback refused to settle for less than they were worth.

Another role model I had during that time was a girl I had recently became friends with. Her free-spirited nature awed me and her love of the little intricacies in life really helped me greater appreciate the things I should be grateful for. She was someone I really looked toward at this point in my life, although I've never told her this.

Every time I woke up in a panic at 11pm and went to grab my phone to text my ex, I would take a moment, lay back and think about things with more clarity.

Using my chosen role model and their strong behaviors, I let them guide me. I wouldn't have the strength they do or achieve things like them if I caved so easily; these role models

#3 Daily mini goals

Days off work would mean I had plenty of time on my hands. Often shutting myself away, I'd run the risk (certainty almost) of contacting my ex.

It was days like this that I needed mini goals.

Instead of spending the day in bed, I'd create a list the night before of small goals I needed to complete the next day. Although spending the day in bed is normal after a break-up (necessary some may say!), when I knew I was going to be especially prone to picking up the phone, I'd assert myself into being productive.

A daily mini list could look like this (taken from my own journal):

8am – Wake up
8.30am - Have a healthy breakfast today

9am – Walk the dog (at least an hour)

10.30am - Empty spare room and declutter

12pm – Make lunch and watch some uplifting videos on YouTube

2pm – Walk the dog (again, at least an hour!)

3.30pm - Pick up some groceries

4pm – Read – magazines, books, newspapers

6pm – Have a bath and unwind

7.30pm - Check e-mails

8pm – Set up new computer desk for office

10pm – Sleep

As mundane and boring it may seem, keeping a regimented schedule of my free time ensured I was always keeping my mind busy with other things. They may seem tedious, but each of them made sure my mind was active with other things; making lunch, engaging in some reading, setting up furniture and getting inspired by YouTube videos.

Wine at the end of the day was a welcome reward for using the willpower I summoned by setting myself mini goals.

I suggest, if you can, you buy a special journal to document this and ensure you keep it with you.

You should reward yourself, too; it's certainly no easy feat to maintain zero contact after a hard break-up. You will get there, though – don't doubt it!

Interlude

When you were younger and imagining how your life would pan out with your soul mate, I can offer a good guess that what you're going through right now isn't what you had in mind. So, the next affirmation aims to solidify that you shouldn't allow something so undeserving to consume your thoughts.

"I deserve better"

You deserve better treatment, someone who wants to be with you and who would absolutely fight for you. You deserve better. Once you realize this, you can begin attracting the things that you DO deserve into your life.

CHAPTER 4

Breaking Bad ... Habits

The mix of rejection and loss you feel after a break-up is almost too great to put into words descriptive enough.

These two elements can send your emotional hardwiring into overdrive and leave you aghast with crippling anxiety.

They also lead to bad habits that have arisen to quell these unwanted feelings of anxiety, frustration and despair. The thing about these bad habits is that you need to suffer the angst of creating them before you quash them – there is no sliding past these bad habits during a break up.

The good news is that to eradicate these bad habits, you need to recognize them, and that's easier to do when you can read the below break-up bad habits and apply them to yourself.

Bad Habit #1 – Not socializing

I did it myself – laid in bed or on the sofa too many days to count. Days would trickle into nights and I'd only move to go to the bathroom or grab a drink; not always a soft one, either. I wouldn't eat and going to sleep would mean I suffered horrible dreams, often about the break-up. I'd wake up in a panic and feel physically sick. I couldn't face anyone; not that I really wanted to either.

What can be worse is going out and being reminded of happier times with your ex. It could be particular bars, places, smells or sounds that just trigger your emotions.

I recall being in a store and seeing the DVD on sale of the last film we watched at the cinema together. I remember us laughing as we watched the movie together and the warm summer night air that hit us as we walked home that evening.

I felt incredibly sick and just darted home, wondering if I could ever just function as a normal person again. At that time, it certainly didn't seem like it.

I found it so difficult to even leave the house, let alone speak to people.

If you're feeling this way too, and are avoiding people, I would stress that this is going to make things harder for you in the long run. Taking these difficult first steps of socializing now will really help speed up this healing process.

Having been in this hard situation, I fully understand that you don't want to see or speak to people. At the same time, you've sought out help by reading this, so I will offer some advice below and I urge you to give them a go …

Seek out existing friends

Have some people in particular been trying to reach out to you? And have you been shunning their attempts?

It's true that some people will just try and contact you for some gossip or because they are nosey; however, it's important to remember that there are good, decent and genuine people out there who are concerned and who can help.

Put a close friend of yours in the position you're in now – would you want to be able to be there for them and help out in any which way you could? I recommend you let your friends in, even if you feel you're at your worst and can't face anybody. I understand you feel it's humiliating and you'd rather avoid them seeing you so helpless, but this is your ego getting in the way of something that can help you feel much better.

A true friend will only want to help, so please don't worry about getting judged.

Consider reconnecting with old friends

Letting go of friends when in a relationship is such a heartbreakingly common thing, especially if you are in a abusive or volatile relationship.

Twice in my life I have let go of friends because my partners of choice didn't like them. The reasons for me having to drop my friends for good differed – I had to drop one because I 'became someone different when I was with her, another I had to drop because they were single and would lead me astray ... pretty soon I was left with nobody but my then-partner.

I was in a state of weakness and I was allowing somebody else to control my life. I was fearful of being alone, so I was allowing myself to be manipulated and isolated – how ironic.

Does this sound like you too?

If so, I urge you to reconnect with old friends. I swallowed my pride and got back in touch with a few of the people I'd let go of during my relationships. Granted, it was hard at first. I was totally honest with them about my reasoning for dropping off the face of the earth, and I was wholly apologetic.

I didn't expect these friendships to regain the strength they once had, but I was pleasantly surprised for the most part. It was cathartic to meet up with these old friends and be completely honest about everything.

To be greeted with forgiveness, empathy and a renewed friendship was unexpected but it ended up being the general reaction to my reconnection with lost friends.

I can't promise this will be the case if you do reach out to old friends, but at least you know you've attempted to make amends and can move on. Don't take this rejection to heart – learn from it, and carry on.

Seek out new friends

It's a daunting prospect, isn't it? Making new friends can be difficult at the best of times, let alone when you are still hurt and reeling from a relationship that has ended.

I know it seems almost too much to live your life like normal, let alone with added friendships, but I absolutely recommend being open to seeking out new friendships.

You can do this online or in person. You can meet people who share the same interests, hobbies, likes, goals, ideas … there's never been such an easy time to make friends when you have a laptop or a smartphone. There are apps to help you connect with people, forums, groups, courses ... just see what's out there.

I've done this. I was totally still broken hearted, and sought out someone who was going through a similar time in their life. We connected via a website and met up for a drink. As I said, I was still taking the break-up very hard and proceeded to get drunk and cut short our first meet; luckily this person was going through the same and understood.

Over the next few weeks we would meet up, talk, swap stories and help each other pull through. I didn't have this person in my life very long, however; she decided the best way to overcome her break-up was to go travelling. So, off she went. I admired her guts, and we still keep connected via Facebook so I can see she's doing great for herself.

So, put yourself out there! Even if you don't feel like meeting up with anyone just yet, try and get to know someone else and you'll be amazed at how much better they can make you feel.

Don't sit and dwell alone – there's only so much feeling sorry for yourself allowed!

It may sound a little harsh – but there is only so much feeling sorry for yourself you can do! You may even read that and think *"I'm heartbroken – how can you just say I'm feeling sorry for myself?!"* … and I understand that. I've been there.

But there comes a time when you need to dig deep, take control and carry yourself to where you need to be.

Sitting at home every day and not socializing isn't going to end your pain, nor is sitting contemplating the ins and outs of your relationship.

Counter your negative thoughts and feelings with positive actions. Remember you are valuable and worthwhile, no matter what happened. Isolating yourself for long periods of time isn't going to help you in this situation. Even if you take tiny steps towards socializing, it'll benefit you in much bigger ways.

Bad Habit #2 – Thinking of Revenge

The overwhelming thoughts of revenge are ugly, it's hard to deny – but we are all human and it takes guts to admit that we have them. If you're not careful, it can be all-consuming, depending on the circumstances of the break-up. If you were cheated on or worse, chances are, you'll have thought of a thing or two to teach your ex a lesson.

I'll admit I was guilty of this also. Like I say, we are all human and this is part of the healing process. Hurtful revenge isn't something that would cross my mind today, but we all go through those dark phases and come out a much better person when the dust of the break-up settles.

The thing that most of the broken-hearted forget is that you *can* extract revenge, as long as you don't go looking for it. If you focus solely on you, your own health, wealth and happiness, you'll be organically creating a strong, attractive figure that would make your ex pale in comparison.

This bittersweet revenge is a by-product of learning to love yourself, a little dose of karma perhaps.

By focusing on you, this would mean you are laying the foundations to become better than the person you were whilst you were in the relationship. Of course, this will stir up several emotions in your ex; jealousy, envy, wanting you back or trying to contact you. By this point however, when you are focused solely on you, your future and who is now in your life, it won't matter.

The best 'revenge' is getting over your ex and having a happy, fulfilled life whilst constantly growing as a person.

I must point out, however, that you can't make this your goal in your mission towards bettering yourself, otherwise you'll have already failed. Focus on you, and things will fall into place.

I do understand the feeling of pain and rejection rearing its head in the form of wanting to extract revenge. TV shows and films even promote the idea as being a good one! I can assure you, revenge isn't a good idea.

Use the fuel of wanting revenge and change it into a positive. Think about where you want to be in six months' time, one years' time, three years' time... where will you be in life, what steps are you going to take to obtain that dream job, house, car, lifestyle?

Whenever you get the restless urge to think about revenge, refocus that energy and swap your thoughts to something more positive that focuses on you. I know it sounds hard to do, but once you've practiced it a few times, it gets easier. And once you're thinking about where you need to be and the steps needed to get there, it's like a domino effect of ideas. One thought leads to another and eventually your ideas start becoming plans.

Small steps like this can really add up to becoming major leaps forward in your journey to healing your broken heart and moving on to become better.

Interlude

The next affirmation allows you to be completely human yet remain strong-willed at the same time. It was one of my favorite affirmations during my break-up:

I will grieve this relationship, but I won't wallow in it.

I found this affirmation allowed me to accept the fact that I *will* feel low whilst I worked at getting over the relationship, but it instilled strength in me at the same time. It reaffirmed to me that whilst I know I'm only human, I am also better than this and I won't let it sink me; I will not wallow.

I think finding strength out of things that can be perceived as weakness is one of life's ironic beauties.

Give yourself the understanding and compassion to grieve the loss of the relationship, but don't let that descend into wallowing. Have the strength and love for yourself to say "enough is enough" when the desire to wallow takes over.

I understand, it's much easier said than done. But once you begin to affirm this aloud and take action upon it, you'll be drawing upon strength you didn't know you had. Eventually, these affirmations will begin to resonate into your subconscious and will be integrated into your mind.

It takes time, but practicing these affirmations does help.

Bad Habit #3 – Drinking too much

I was absolutely guilty of this bad habit. Even thinking about the days when I would use alcohol as a coping mechanism makes me feel hungover. The amount I would drink would be embarrassing to admit but clear to see from all the empty bottles laying around my kitchen.

I mostly drank to blot out pain and help me sleep without having nightmares. Without alcohol, if it wasn't nightmares, I'd get those awful dreams where my ex and I got back together and I would wake up and believe it for the first ten seconds I opened my eyes. The heart-dropping, gut-churning realization that I was no longer wanted by my ex would then hit me.

It was one of the most agonizing emotional pains I had ever experienced.

Using alcohol to cope with the pain of a break-up is common, but it's also damaging.

We'll all have our blow-outs and drunken sobs to songs that remind us of our ex, but using alcohol to dull our thoughts and emotions frequently will become harmful.

If you feel you're drinking too much, it's a great first step simply recognizing that there may be an issue. The next step is to then give yourself a good shake and start to take back control of your emotions. By using alcohol to 'ease' you through this turbulent time, you're self-medicating and going down a self-destructive route – now is the time to take charge of your emotions and deal with them.

After all, alcohol is a depressant when you use it the wrong way.

When I accepted that alcohol was becoming a problem, it was much later than everyone else. Friends and family had warned me gently about it becoming an issue, but I didn't listen. I even headed to the pub on my lunch break at work occasionally, and continued my binge when I returned home.

It eventually got to the point that other aspects of my life were crumbling around me, like my job. I knew I needed to take action and pouring my bottle down the drain was the first thing I did.

When you feel the urge to use drink as a way to cope with your feelings during this time, I would suggest you think about the bigger picture. Using alcohol to dull, eradicate or misplace your emotions is only prolonging the pain of the break-up and possibly set you back, leaving you vulnerable and perhaps trying to contact them.

Trust me, even if you delete the cringe-worthy texts the next morning, you still sent them!

I replaced all alcohol in my house with healthy juices and water and practiced eradicating the negative urges to drink. I did this by refocusing my mind on me and in my most fragile moments would repeat my positive affirmations to myself.

I'm not suggesting you don't drink, but be extra vigilant during this tough emotional time. If you need to, confide in a trusted friend or family member.

Bad Habit #4 – Random Hooking Up

I recall a friend telling me during my last break-up that the best way to get over my ex was to sleep with someone new. At first, I winced and cringed at the idea of being with anybody but my ex.

But then I began seeing things on social media (often the enemy of the broken hearted – refer back to chapter two!) … that deeply upset me. I could see he was moving on, and with different girls. As well as the hurtful pictures, I could also see all of the comments he was making. I barely recognized it was him – he never spoke to me the way he did his new girlfriends.

It was after seeing this, I decided to act on my friend's advice. I slept with someone new. I met this person on a dating app and they lived in my city. I felt awful afterwards.

I wasn't suddenly 'cured' of my broken heart nor were any of my feelings for my ex disappearing – in fact, this new encounter only made me want to feel the comfort and familiarity of my ex even more.

I'd listened to some bad advice from a good friend who meant well – but it really did backfire. After this experience, I couldn't imagine going near anybody else again!

Intuition, your heart and your head will tell you when it's time to hook up with somebody new. I did this way too soon and with completely the wrong person.

For some people, meeting new people, sleeping with them and then moving on is a way of coping. In reality, these people are numbing the real pain of their break-up and letting it fester inside whilst they get a quick fix of feeling wanted.

After the rejection of a relationship being ended, it's easy to see how this trap is an easy one to fall into. If you are feeling like moving on with new people is going to help you forget your ex, I can assure you it won't – not for long, anyhow. Those few moments of being with somebody new will only make the thoughts, comparisons and memories of your ex all that more intense.

It all comes back to putting yourself first. You are worth more than a few lousy hookups that will only make you feel devalued in the long run. Instead of thinking about the short-term fix of getting with someone new, devote that time, thought and energy to yourself. You won't become who you need to become when you are considering giving yourself away to quash the hurt of your break-up.

Will the you in twelve months' time look back and think "hooking up with that random guy was such a good idea"? Your chances are slim.

In keeping with the theme of the past few bad habits, again I'm going to advise you to forget about partaking in this break-up bad habit and focus on *you*. I know it feels unbearably lonely, but please have faith that you can and will come out of this happier and with more self-esteem than before. Running into the arms of someone new is a toxic distraction.

Again, when these self-destructive ideas come into play, it's a good idea to think about you and where you want to be in your life. Do you want to get a specific job, do you want to have your own business, do you want to move to a certain location?

When I began talking back to my destructive behavior, it was then that I started making little steps towards bettering myself. I started taking night classes to work towards my psychology degree, I became more assertive at work and begun saying "no" when I was being taken for granted and I had the rest of my year planned.

I used the negative and destructive emotions I was feeling and channeled them aggressively into bettering myself.

Before I knew it, I looked back at the previous few months and was mightily proud of myself. In what felt like the blink of an eye, I had used the anger, fear and resentment that had built up inside me and let it fuel my positive actions.

Bad Habit #5 – Idealizing the Relationship

This bad habit is without a doubt a sure-fire way to keep you stuck where you are; trapped in your emotional prison with the thoughts of your ex and the relationship you once had consuming your mind.

The ironic thing here is that you hold the key to unlocking your prison cell door. The worst thing is that most broken-hearted people can't see this; they envision their ex dangling those keys just outside of arms reach through the cell door. The truth is the keys are within your grasp.

Idealizing an ex means that you're replaying all of the nice moments you both shared in your head and recounting every positive interaction.

Of course, when you've shared such an intimate bond with somebody and have opened up to them, it's completely natural to fall into the trap of idealizing them and the relationship you had. Don't beat yourself up after a bout of thinking about the good times. Know that it's natural, but remind yourself of the following:

- When we idealize an ex, we see them for something they weren't: perfect.
- If we see our ex as perfect, then it creates a perfect distraction from facing grief. By placing a dark shadow over our head, we are putting off accepting the real reasons for the break-up. No matter the reasons why or your part in the break-up – avoid casting this dark cloud over yourself.
- Developing these idealistic thoughts can turn into more serious, obsessive thoughts. We do this to push away the real grief that the partnership is over. By becoming obsessive over how perfect and ideal your ex was, it helps soften the pain that you feel when you face up to the truth of reality.

When you face prolonged periods of idealizing your ex, and you feel like these thoughts are all-consuming, I'd suggest that you take pen to paper. Again, you don't need to keep this after you've jotted it down, although it could be good for future reference. Write down the facts as they happened – they good, the bad and the ugly. Include things you did wrong, things they did wrong. Include happier days on this timeline also.

Spend as long as you need doing this.

The point of this exercise is to take a sober, cold, hard look at the relationship. To ensure your thoughts aren't just engulfed with overly positive or negative thoughts about your ex. By completing the above task, you'll experience different emotions that will help you free your thoughts from your idealistic views.

Interlude

"The only person I have control over is myself."

This affirmation can, at first, be heartbreaking. The fact that you can't make someone love you when you just know you'd be great for them is gut-sinking.

As you grieve the end of the relationship, it's highly important that you offer doses of reality to yourself from time to time. Affirmations like the one above will really hit home – we don't have control over our ex's actions. What they are doing now, and whoever they are doing it with, is of their own free will.

You have no power to stop them doing that.

What you **can,** and must control, is yourself.

It's within your power to let go, heal yourself and move on to bigger and better things.

CHAPTER 5

Learning Self-Care

The most important things we forget about during the aftermath of a break-up is who we are, what we want and what we deserve. In a nutshell, we forget to take care of ourselves.

This is where the art of self-care comes in.

Self-care means actively choosing behaviors to balance (and not bury) the effects of the stresses that this break-up has caused you.

Self-care is a soothing and productive way to ease yourself out of the shackles of the break-up and truly find yourself again. Oftentimes, the broken-hearted end up becoming a much better version of themselves than they ever thought possible when they chose to learn some self-care techniques – this can be true for you, too. It was certainly true for me, and I was at a very, very low ebb after my relationship ended.

I recall saying to a friend at the time of the split, *"I would just be happy to feel nothing, as long as I don't feel like this anymore"*. I look back and I'm astounded by the grit and determination that can be derived from such pain and heartache. I'm even more astounded by the resolve of our emotions as humans – we're capable of so much more than we give ourselves credit for.

I'm proud of myself for really turning my ship around. You can look forward to your proud moments, too; there will be a few, but none as exhilarating as the time you finally look back on your emotional rollercoaster and see just how well you're doing now.

With some self-care, learning to be easy on yourself and following the advice laid out earlier in the book, you will be taking steps towards becoming the person you deserve to be.

Self-care isn't as big or as daunting as it may initially sound; in fact, when you're practicing self-care, it may not feel like you're doing much at all. Some days, self-care may feel like a breeze, other days the smallest act of taking care of yourself will seem too difficult to comprehend.

This section of the book will give you the tools to not just help you function the right way again, but it will also help you flourish.

I categorize each self-care technique under three umbrellas; mind, body and soul.

Mind

Respecting your mind is an important part of being. Unfortunately, it's something most people tend to forget to focus on, let alone those who are experiencing the emotional carnage of a break-up. Here are some techniques to help you recharge your mind – give a few of these ago this week, and you'll subconsciously be giving your mind a bit of TLC.

#1 - Disconnect for an hour: Put your phone on airplane mode, unplug your telephone, shut down your laptop ... completely let your mind unwind. Try listening to the birds outside, the rain on the windows, the sirens or traffic outside. Go where your mind takes you.

#2 - Switch up your route to work: Even if it takes you a little longer to get there, or you need to set off a little earlier. This little technique is a subconscious way to keep your mind healthy. The neural pathways in your brain will have a good response to this unusual change in routine.

#3 - Be selfish: Make this one a priority – do one thing a day (at least) just for you, because it makes you happy.

#4 - Declutter: It could be your wardrobe, your ex's things, your office table … it's amazing what a physical declutter can do for your mind. I decluttered my spare room and turned it into a neat little office space and it became a passion project as well as much needed productive distraction.

#5 - Remove yourself from your comfort zone: Even if it's striking up a conversation at the office with someone you've never chatted to or partaking in a meeting – get your mind out of its comfort zone! You'll thank yourself later.

#6- Social media weed: Anything or anyone negative within your social media feeds, weed them out. It will only reinforce your mind that it needs to continue with its negative thought patterns. If you don't want to delete someone, you can 'mute' them for now.

#7 - People watch: It's amazing the inspiration you give your mind simply by sitting at a coffee shop and watching the world around you. Even if you are hesitant to go to a coffee shop alone, do it (see #5 about getting out of your comfort zone).

Body

#1 – Deep breaths: Inhale for six seconds, exhale for seven. Repeat this three times. Oxygenating your body really can take the edge of stress, anxiety and panic.

#2 – Drink herbal / green teas: Not only are green and herbal teas a great way to flush toxins out of your body, you can inhale their upbeat scents. I enjoy peppermint tea and combining it with some light reading.

#3 – Change up your food choices: Pick just two healthy breakfasts, lunches and dinners for your week. Stick to these and try and keep up with drinking two liters of water a day. It's amazing how looking after your insides like this can have such a positive impact on your emotional wellbeing – but it really does.

#4 – Give your body a treat: A comforting, nourishing body moisturizer or a new shower wash can make you feel better. It can also help aid that all-important good night's sleep that is needed more than normal when you're going through the trauma of a break-up. Indulge in yourself a little.

#5 – Take a walk / go for a run: Apart from the well-known endorphins that exercise releases in your brain, it'll also be a positive for your physical health. Depending on where you are physically, run or walk – even just do laps of your stairs on really difficult days. It's important that you do this technique as it's important to your wellbeing, even if you need to lay your running gear out the night before or set an alarm before work. I would walk my dog miles from my city house to the country, so it also did him a world of good too!

#6 – Turn on some upbeat music: Until you find yourself having a bit of a dance. Even go full blown boogie if you can! Maybe you can have a declutter and accompany this with some music or the radio; you'll be taking on two acts of self-care without even realizing. Uplifting your spirits and allowing your mind to think *"okay, I'm gonna get myself through this"* isn't as painstaking as you may think – the hardest part is just getting started and taking action.

#7 – Go outside: Get some sun if you can. Go sit on a park bench or go somewhere green if possible. Just let the clouds above you pass you by and breathe in the fresh air around you, letting your mind wander where it wants.

Soul

#1 – Help someone else: You may be thinking that you can barely help yourself right now, so how can you begin to help someone else? It only takes small gestures; helping someone carry their heavy shopping to their car or doing the milk run at work. Be kind, and you will be rewarded, even though it doesn't feel that way now.

#2 – Date yourself: Yep, you did read that correctly. Have a date night with yourself. Light a few candles, put on some soothing music, cook yourself a nice dinner (or order takeout – it's nice to indulge!) and watch a movie or settle down with a good book. Making yourself content doesn't need to be as hard as you think – give this a go.

#3 – Seek out beauty everywhere: On your way home from work or whilst out shopping, take yourself on a beauty scavenger hunt. Look out for the intricacies and form of things and find the beauty in them. Make it your goal to find five things of beauty on your next outing.

#4 – Take a break: Alone. Even if it's just a day out in your city or a nearby town, take yourself away for a day or two. Explore, indulge, be inquisitive and open to new experiences. It's time alone like this that we can really get to know ourselves that much better, and taking a big step out of your comfort zone like this is a positive step for the mind. You don't need to spend much money doing this, either.

#5 – If you need help, ask for it: Whether you're at work or talking to your credit card company, it does wonders for your soul when you swallow your anxiety and ask for help. To push forward to positivity, you need to know that everyone needs help from time to time. You'll feel so much better once your stresses are out in the open, and you'll begin to feel like you can get on top of things.

#6 – Keep a thought diary: In keeping with other parts of this book, writing your thoughts and feelings down is a very cathartic way of releasing negative emotions. Remember that journal I suggested keeping earlier on? Here is another great use for it. At the end of every day, you should make note of how you've felt that day; any highs, lows or in-betweens. Then end your daily diary of how you wish to feel tomorrow and how you could achieve that.

#7 – Reach out with small gestures: Things like engaging with the barista who serves you your coffee or smiling at someone fills up your soul with positive energy. Even if this doesn't sound like you and you usually shy away from doing these kinds of little gestures, I urge you to give them a go – you'll feel a little better after each one.

With each little bit of attention you give to you and your self-care is a leap in the right direction for where you want to be heading in life.

After you have tended to yourself piece by piece, you'll eventually feel the fog lifting from above you. You'll have spent time and care nourishing yourself and the techniques above will help you feel more connected to yourself than ever.

With each small step being taking, things won't seem as difficult as they did before. You can even create your own self-care routines; waking up early to have a run, eating a healthy breakfast and ensuring you take chances to step out of your comfort zone where possible – whatever works best for you and your situation.

Take inspiration from the above and begin to practice small actions that will soon begin to resonate as healthy habits. These will enable you to begin rising from the black hole of heartbreak into a world of hopefulness, positivity and happiness.

CHAPTER 6

Moving On

It's amazing to look back on my life and see how far I've come, and in such a short space of time in reality. I'm already excited for you to reach that moment!

From being utterly devastated and beyond heartbroken to now living a life of happiness, working for myself and meeting the love of my life, I have not only found myself again – I've become a better version of myself.

By recognizing the stages of a break-up, understanding that I had to abstain from contact, severing ties with my bad habits and learning self-care, I was able to come out of the other side of this low period. And it was only because I worked at the above that I was able to enter into another relationship again.

Meeting my current partner was highly unexpected and I certainly wasn't searching for it.

In fact, I had solid plans in place, all of which didn't include meeting somebody and falling in love. Serendipity at its finest.

When I met my partner, my plans were all very 'me' central – the way it needed to be after my heartbreaking split. I had plans in place to move to London, I had already relocated to a lovely, old house for the time being (to help escape memories from the one I shared with my ex) and I had taken up a few new hobbies.

I found life exciting again. I was looking forward to new experiences, opportunities and places.

Then, as soon as I was well and truly back on my feet, this person came into my life and blew me away.

I was very cautious; I was doing fantastically well for myself and didn't want to be heartbroken again. The fact that I had already overcome such heartache proved to me that I could get over a break-up – I just didn't want to have to go through that again. So, up my walls went.

I was incredibly hard work; I was emotionally unavailable and mistrusting. At the same time, however, I was mesmerized by this being. And they were with me, too; it was confusing and exciting at the same time.

To help you avoid the same mistakes I made when meeting someone new after a break-up, I'd like to share some advice on behaviors to encourage and discourage when you meet someone who you can see yourself being with.

Tip #1 – Be Honest

Of course, I don't mean spilling your guts about all of the tragedies that have befallen you over the course of your lifetime on date number one. But, be honest about the fact that you've been hurt and that your previous relationship left you emotionally damaged and drained.

Share your truth. It will also enable your prospective partner to be a little more understanding when you're perhaps being a little colder than you were the last time they seen you, or it may explain mistrustful emotions.

Whilst you may feel vulnerable and open to hurt by being honest, it's always the best way to start out a new relationship. If you go into this new venture full of bravado, falseness and an *"I don't care"* attitude, you could end up ruining something that could have been good for you. Not only that, you run the risk of hurting someone who put themselves out there for you.

I did this to my current partner – my bravado and visible lack of care really did run them to the ground.

Deep down, however, I was enamored with this person and looking back I regret not being as honest with them – it would have saved months of wasted emotion and time.

Tip #2 – Be You

Even if you think you're too weird, too loud, too quiet, too whatever – be you. It's the most attractive thing a person can be when opposite the *right* person.

I'm naturally quirky with quite a dry sense of humor, and I was worried this might be off-putting for my (then) new partner. Still, I decided to remain who I was because if that side of me put them off, then it wasn't meant to be anyhow.

It turns out that my quirks and oddities were something my new partner found attractive, and after several dates together, I picked up that he had very similar quirks and a dry sense of humor. He now admits he was afraid to show this side of him too early as he didn't want to scare me off.

Image how much fun we missed out on in the beginning when he wasn't being true to himself or me?

The advice here is to just be you, no matter what.

Tip #3 – Be Adventurous

With a new significant other, try something neither of you has ever done before. Create new memories and don't be afraid to do so in case this relationship doesn't work out. A life lived in fear isn't a life worth living, after all – get out there and be adventurous!

Remember earlier when I said change stimulates your brain to make you happier? It's something you ought to keep in mind, and the beginning of a new relationship is a great time to be adventurous and change things up.

I don't necessarily mean jump out of a plane with your new beau (although you absolutely could), but trying new things together is a fantastic way to help ease you back into emotional fulfillment with another person and stimulate your mind.

Why not try a cooking class together, go wine tasting, visit a drive-thru cinema or take a trip to a theme park?

Tip #4 – Be Open

This is uber important – you can't shut yourself down because you've had bad experiences. I've overcome domestic and emotional abuse and still found it within myself to open up to somebody new. Whatever you have experienced or been through, I know you can open up, too.

Putting defenses up when we are faced with a prospect that may hurt us in the future is natural. It's what your mind does to avoid the danger of repeating the emotional trauma you went through with your ex.

However, to go into a new relationship when you are unwilling to be open is likely to only end one way; you'll end up hurting the other person.

I suggest that you don't allow the heartache of the past affect your openness with your new suitor. As hard as it may be at first, when you begin to feel your barriers rising you need to explain this to your partner and actively work at breaking them down.

Don't hide away from your partner – this was a huge mistake I made at the beginning of my current relationship. As I said before, I look back now and see my time as being reserved and closed down towards my partner as wasted time. Even if it never worked out between us, having that guard so far up would have served no purpose – it would have also meant I hadn't given then relationship my all.

Tip #5 – Have Fun

The more fun you have without a significant other, the more fun you can have with the one that finally gets your heart.

In fact, I think this is the way I found my partner – I was busy having fun. I was collecting new friends, memories, living in new places and even having a lot of success networking for my job.

I was so busy growing, having fun and genuinely enjoying myself. My partner seen this and it intrigued him. I can't say he'd have felt the same if I was downbeat, full of resentment and holding onto the anger of my break-up.

Although you may feel it's too difficult to "have fun" right now, if you give yourself time and go through the steps outlined in the chapters above, you'll find yourself having fun without realizing it; one day you'll be in high spirits and enjoying yourself and it'll dawn upon you that you're actually having *fun*.

These moments will become more frequent until you don't need to document them in your head. You'll simply be having fun.

Tip #6 – Be Careful

This may seem a little contradictory to some of the points above or a little bit of a buzzkill, but hear me out.

Yes, you need to be open and honest, but you also need to listen to your gut. Check in with your feelings and listen to what your gut tells you.

Does this person mirror characteristics of your ex and that's what's drawing you towards them? Alternatively, are they the complete opposite of your ex and that's the only reason you're leaning towards them? Perhaps you're ignoring warning signs because you don't want to have a failed relationship or you're focusing too much on things which then causes problems?

I'm not suggesting you mull over every intricacy of the new relationship, but it's wise to maintain your emotional integrity, and that means being real with yourself. It'll save both you and your new love interest heartache in the long run if you can weed out any potential disasters before they arise.

I believe you will overcome this break-up and prosper.

I have given you the mental tools I used to overcome my heartache and shared pieces of my story with you in hopes you will take inspiration from it, or find some familiarity in it at the very least.

I also wrote this book to offer comfort, to let you know that you're not alone and that this terrible time in your life will pass. I hope I have given you a better understanding of what you now need to do in order to get past this break-up and on to much better things.

I offer you my sincere wishes of health, wealth and happiness. I know that it's all within your reach if you tough out the hard stuff during this time.

If there is anything you feel I have missed out or if there's any feedback you would like to offer about this book, please go ahead and leave me a review. If you're comfortable doing so, perhaps you can leave a little backstory about your break-up in your review and offer some hope to those also experiencing a break-up. If you found this little book a help, a good source of advice and / or a comforting read, then please let me know by adding a review. It would be so appreciated.

As a bonus chapter, I've compiled my favorite 'break-up' quotes. I hope they give you some food for thought.

Here's to getting over your break-up and moving on to better things. I know you will do it.

Robin Martel

Interlude

"I am going to heal."

Bonus Chapter

Please read these and take the time to ponder each one.

Relate it to your situation and your circumstances.

Think about what the quote means and how that is relevant to you. Let the wise words of others who have been where you are guide you forward.

Loving someone who doesn't love you is like waiting for a ship at the airport.

If you can love the wrong person that much, imagine how much you can love the right one.

If you were happy with the wrong one, just imagine how happy you'll be with the right one.

You cannot let go of someone you never really had, and if you had them you wouldn't have to let go.

We must be willing to let go of the life we planned in order to have the life that is waiting for us.

When one door closes, another opens; but we often look so long and so regretfully upon the closed door that we do not see the one which has opened for us.

Made in the USA
Columbia, SC
07 March 2018